A is for Amazing
Students - Ryan

June 2014

This has been an Amazing year, with Amazing students that I will never forget. I loved this book for each of you because I know you are capable of achieving Amazing things in life. Keep your heads held high and reach for the stars. Have an Amazing summer!

Love, *Mrs. Delaney*

A is for Amazing Moments

A Sports Alphabet

Written by Brad Herzog and Illustrated by Melanie Rose

Sleeping Bear Press™

310 North Main Street, Suite 300
Chelsea, MI 48118
www.sleepingbearpress.com

© 2008 Sleeping Bear Press is an imprint of Gale, a part of Cengage Learning.

Printed and bound in Canada.

First Edition

10 9 8 7 6 5 4 3 2 1

Library of Congress Cataloging-in-Publication Data

Herzog, Brad.
A is for amazing moments : a sports alphabet / written by Brad Herzog;
illustrated by Melanie Rose.
p. cm.
Summary: "Following the alphabet from A to Z, amazing and memorable
sports moments are introduced with two-tier writing—poems and detailed
side-bar text. Topics include Jackie Robinson's courage; Gertrude Ederle
swimming the English Channel; Bob Beamon's long jump; and Jesse
Owens'Medal of Freedom"—Provided by publisher.
ISBN 978-1-58536-360-5
1. Sports--Juvenile literature. 2. Alphabet books . I. Rose,
Melanie, ill. II. Title.
GV705.4.H47 2008
796—dc22   2008011026

For my brother Brian and my sister Laura,
with whom I've shared many amazing moments.

BRAD

❦

For Norm.

MELANIE

For most of the 1960s, the New York Mets were the worst team in baseball. In their first season, 1962, they lost 120 games (winning only 40), and they finished in last place five more years in a row. But in 1968, things began to improve. The team hired a new manager, Gil Hodges, and found some excellent pitchers, including future Hall of Famers Tom Seaver and Nolan Ryan. Still, the Mets finished in second-to-last place.

But 1969 was a magical season. The Mets improved as the summer moved along, although they were still ten games behind the first-place Chicago Cubs in August. But then the Amazin' Mets (they were also known as the Miracle Mets) began to win like never before— 38 of their last 49 games! They finished first in their division, swept the Atlanta Braves three games to none in the National League playoffs and then beat the heavily favored Baltimore Orioles in the World Series. In their first winning season, the once lowly Mets had won it all!

A

a

After seven awful seasons,
    baseball's Amazin' Mets
        won a shocking World Series title.
That's A in our alphabet.

The Battle of the Sexes.
That's our letter B.
When Billie Jean beat Bobby,
it made for great TV.

Billie Jean King won six Wimbledon tennis championships and four U.S. Open titles, but perhaps her most famous victory came against a 55-year-old man. Bobby Riggs had been the world's top tennis player in the 1940s. By 1973, his game was slower, but his mouth wasn't. Riggs claimed that women's tennis was inferior to the men's game and that the top female players couldn't even beat an older man like himself. So King, then 29 years old and a longtime voice for equal rights, accepted his challenge. In what came to be called the "Battle of the Sexes," she hoped to teach Riggs a lesson, while inspiring women everywhere.

On September 20, 1973, in front of more than 30,000 spectators at the Houston Astrodome and nearly 50 million television viewers, King beat Riggs in three straight sets, 6-4, 6-3, 6-3. "It helped a lot of people realize that everyone can have skills, whether you are a man or woman," she explained.

C is one man's Courage.
Jackie Robinson did his part
by showing skin color doesn't matter.
What counts is in your heart.

Hall of Famer Jackie Robinson is deservedly remembered as the man who broke baseball's color barrier. In 1947 he played for the Brooklyn Dodgers, becoming the first African-American major leaguer of the twentieth century. But fewer people recall his performance as the first African-American minor leaguer one year earlier. Under enormous pressure to show that black players belonged in baseball, Robinson proved to be the best player on the field.

On April 18, 1946, in front of more than 50,000 spectators in Jersey City, New Jersey, Robinson was the second batter of the game for the Montreal Royals of the International League. After letting five pitches go by for a full count, he grounded out to the shortstop. But from then on, he was almost perfect. In his second at-bat, Robinson hit a three-run home run, probably the most significant homer in baseball history. By the end of that game, he had collected four hits, four runs, three runs batted in and two stolen bases. Jackie Robinson had arrived, and the game would never be the same again.

C c

The 1976 Daytona 500 featured a remarkable duel between the two most successful racers in stock car racing history—Richard Petty and David Pearson. After dominating all day, the rivals were running first and second as they entered the final lap. Petty led in Turns 1 and 2. Pearson passed him in Turn 3. Petty eased ahead in Turn 4. But then the front of Pearson's #21 Mercury clipped the right rear of Petty's #43 Dodge, and both cars crashed into the outside wall. Petty's car slid down the track and eventually stalled on the infield grass. Although Pearson's car was still running, he also was slowly sliding out of control. But a third car came by and clipped Pearson, nudging him just enough to turn him in the right direction—toward the finish line 300 yards away. "Here I come! Here I come!" shouted Pearson, and he crossed the finish for his only Daytona 500 victory—at about 20 miles per hour!

D is the Duel at Daytona Speedway
and a dangerous late-race tap.
A crash! A stall! A checkered flag!
What a dramatic final lap!

In the early twentieth century, many people believed that women were incapable of swimming long distances. But a 19-year-old named Gertrude Ederle, who had lost much of her hearing after contracting measles as a child, proved that a woman could best everybody. All she had to do was swim from France to England, something only five men had ever done!

In the early morning of August 6, 1926, Ederle plunged into the English Channel, the body of water separating the two countries. Because stormy weather made it difficult to swim in a straight line, she actually had to swim 35 miles to cross the 21-mile-wide Channel. But she still managed to reach land again 14 hours and 31 minutes later, a faster crossing than anyone had ever recorded. When Ederle returned to her hometown, New York City, some two million people lined the streets for a ticker tape parade.

Nearly three decades later, in 1955, a 17-year-old Canadian named Marilyn Bell became the youngest swimmer to cross the English Channel. One year earlier, she also had become the first woman to swim across 32-mile-wide Lake Ontario.

E
e

E is for the English Channel,
twenty-one miles wide,
and Gertrude Ederle, the first woman
to swim to the other side.

Runners had come oh so close
    and had been trying for quite a while,
    but Roger Bannister finally did it.
F is the first Four-minute mile!

F f

For many years, one athletic feat was considered unreachable—running a mile in under four minutes. Some doctors claimed it was even dangerous to attempt it. But on May 6, 1954, an English medical student put an end to that notion. In front of a small crowd of 1,200 spectators at Oxford University, 25-year-old Roger Bannister made history. With the help of two runners to set the pace for him in the one-mile race, he used a late burst of energy to cross the finish line and fall exhausted into the arms of a friend. His official time: 3 minutes, 59.4 seconds.

With that mental barrier broken, the four-minute-mile became almost commonplace. Within three years, 16 runners broke four minutes, and the current record is nearly 17 seconds faster than Bannister's mark. But Roger Bannister was the first to do it, a feat that many sports historians consider the greatest athletic achievement of all time.

Professional golfers putt on greens, but they like to *put on* the green jacket, which is awarded to the winner of the Masters Tournament at Augusta National Golf Club in Georgia. Two of the most memorable Masters moments were victories for the ages—by the oldest and youngest winners.

By 1986, Jack Nicklaus was already a living legend. But the Golden Bear, as he was called, hadn't won a tournament in two years, and most people thought his best golf was behind him. But the 46-year-old thrilled the gallery by recording an amazing score of 30 on the final nine holes to come from behind and win his record 18th major title and sixth green jacket.

Eleven years later, it was 21-year-old Tiger Woods' turn to thrill the crowds. The youngest Masters champion also set records for the lowest score (18 under par) and largest winning margin (12 strokes!). Tiger was well on his way to catching the Golden Bear.

G g

G is a golfer's Green jacket.
To some, it's worth more than gold.
Tiger and the Golden Bear
were champions, young and old.

H h

A hero hobbled toward home plate.
The home crowd cheered the sight.
H is for a Home Run
hammered far into the night.

There have been many dramatic home runs in baseball, including pennant-winning shots, world championship-winning homers and a clout by 12-year-old Dalton Carriker to take the 2007 Little League World Series. But Kirk Gibson may have provided the most dramatic moment of all.

In Game 1 of the 1988 World Series, the Los Angeles Dodgers trailed the Oakland A's 4-3. There was a runner on first base with two outs in the bottom of the ninth inning. Oakland's Dennis Eckersley, a future Hall of Famer, was on the mound. Then Gibson, who had severe leg injuries and wasn't expected to play at all, limped up to the plate as a pinch hitter. It would be his only at-bat of the series. With the crowd cheering madly and the count full, he took an awkward swing and watched the ball sail into the right field stands. As Gibson pumped his fist while rounding the bases, radio announcer Jack Buck shouted, "I don't believe what I just saw!"

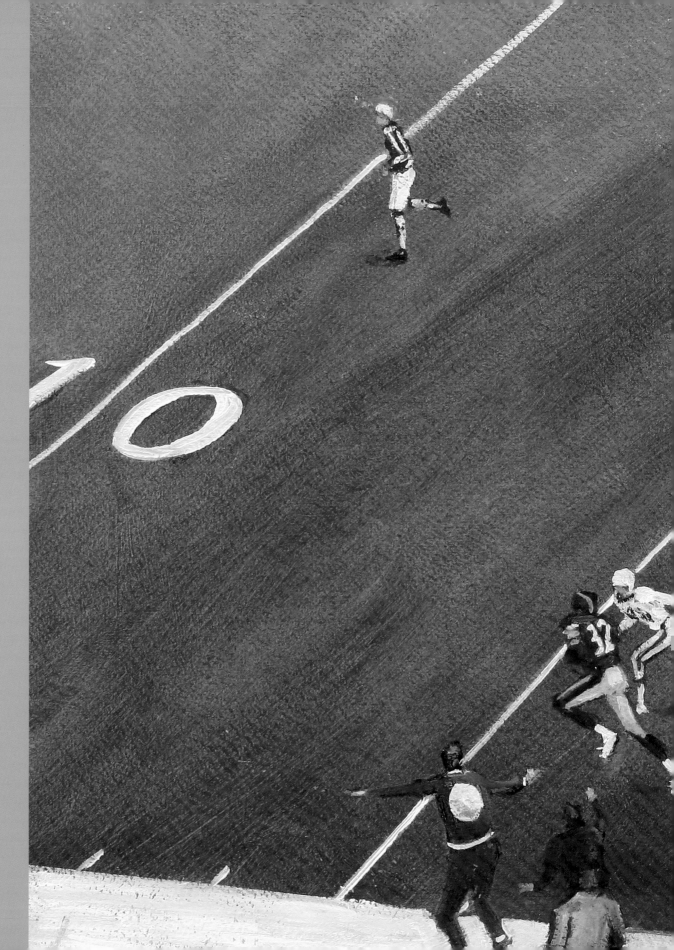

In their first 40 years in the National Football League, the Pittsburgh Steelers never won a playoff game. But one of the most famous plays in football history, jokingly nicknamed the Immaculate Reception (because it wasn't perfect or planned at all), turned the team's fortunes around. On December 23, 1972, Pittsburgh faced the Oakland Raiders in the first round of the playoffs. Down 7-6 with just 22 seconds remaining in the game, the Steelers faced 4th down and 10 yards to go from their own 40-yard line. Quarterback Terry Bradshaw threw a pass to fullback John "Frenchy" Fuqua at the Raiders' 35-yard-line. But just as the football arrived, so did Oakland safety Jack Tatum. The hit sent the ball sailing backwards several yards—right toward Pittsburgh's rookie running back Franco Harris, who scooped it off the top of his shoes and raced downfield for a touchdown! It was an early Christmas gift for Pittsburgh and a long-awaited playoff victory. The Steelers would go on to win four Super Bowls in the next seven seasons.

A playoff game, a desperate pass,
an accidental deflection.
I is for an incredible play,
called the Immaculate Reception.

The incomparable Michael Jordan won ten NBA scoring titles, and he loved to have the basketball in his hands when the game was on the line. Even as a 19-year-old freshman at North Carolina University, he sank a 16-foot jumper to give his Tar Heels the NCAA basketball championship. In his stellar professional career, Jordan produced a game-winning shot an amazing 19 times (and game-winning free throws another six times). But perhaps his most memorable two points were his last points in a Bulls uniform.

In Game 6 of the 1998 Finals, Chicago was losing 86-85 with only seconds remaining. Jordan stole the ball from Utah star Karl Malone, dribbled down the court and calmly sank a 20-foot jump shot with 5.2 seconds left to give Chicago its sixth NBA title in eight years. A perfect ending! "If that's the last image of Michael Jordan," said TV announcer Bob Costas, "how magnificent is it?!"

J j

A Michael Jordan jump shot against the Utah Jazz. His J gave his team the title with typical pizzazz.

K k

K In the World Cup, soccer's big event, must stand for Kick. Brandi Chastain's game-winner is our momentous pick.

It seemed like everyone was watching the finals of the 1999 Women's World Cup soccer match. More than 90,000 fans, including President Bill Clinton, crowded into the Rose Bowl in Pasadena, California. Millions more were glued to their television sets. Meanwhile, Brandi Chastain calmly prepared to attempt the most important kick of her life.

The two teams in this championship match, the United States and China, had played to a 0-0 tie, meaning a shootout would decide the victor. Five players from each team would attempt penalty kicks, one at a time. Chastain was the last American to take a turn. By then, one of the Chinese players had missed her attempt, so a goal would mean a championship for the U.S. team. She set the ball down, stepped back, took a deep breath... and promptly booted the ball into the left corner of the net! Chastain immediately dropped to her knees in celebration. It was, she said, "the greatest moment of my life on the soccer field."

When astronaut Neil Armstrong walked on the moon in 1969, he called it "one giant leap for mankind." But mankind's most famous leap actually occurred one year earlier at the 1968 Summer Olympics in Mexico City, Mexico, when 22-year-old American Bob Beamon made what has been called The Perfect Jump. He took 19 strides down the runway, hurled himself into the air, stretched out his legs in front of him and landed an incredible 29 feet, 2 inches away. He had broken the record by more than 21 inches!

When the announcer called out the distance, Beamon was so astonished that he collapsed to his knees and placed his hands over his face. His record stood until American Mike Powell beat it by two inches in 1991, but Beamon's distance remains the Olympic record —and certainly his personal best. In fact, he never again cleared even 27 feet in competition. But in one great leap, he achieved what many had thought was impossible.

L₁

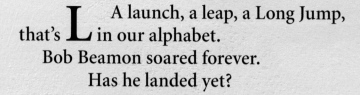

A launch, a leap, a Long Jump,
that's L in our alphabet.
Bob Beamon soared forever.
Has he landed yet?

M m

At the 1980 Winter Olympics in Lake Placid, New York, the United States hockey team wasn't expected to win any medals. But this group of college-aged amateurs would captivate an entire country. Led by coach Herb Brooks, team captain Mike Eruzione and goaltender Jim Craig, the Americans unexpectedly won four games to advance to the medal round. There they faced a team from a country then known as the Soviet Union, a squad that had beaten a group of NHL all-stars 6-0 one year earlier. Observers gave the Americans no chance.

But something magical happened. Eruzione's goal in the third period put his team ahead 4-3, and the Americans held off the Soviets for the final ten minutes, as the crowd cheered deliriously. The U.S. would go on to defeat Finland 4-2 in the final game to win an improbable—almost impossible—gold medal. "Do you believe in miracles?" TV sportscaster Al Michaels asked as the clock ticked to zero against the Soviets. "Yes!"

M A team of unknown college stars outscored a hockey power. M is the Miracle on Ice, the U.S. team's finest hour.

Canadian hockey has its own Miracle on Ice. It happened in the 1972 Summit Series, an eight-game series between the national teams from Canada and the Soviet Union. In the first four games, all played in Canada, the Canadians won only once and tied once. Then the teams traveled to the Soviet Union for the final four contests, and the home team won the fifth game to take a 3-1-1 lead in the series. It didn't look promising for Canada.

Then the miracles began. Canada recorded one-goal victories in Game 6 and Game 7 to tie the series. In the eighth and final game, the Soviets took a 5-3 lead into the third period, but the Canadians soon tied it up. Then, with only 34 seconds remaining and with nearly everyone in Canada watching on television, Canada's Paul Henderson poked in a rebound for the game-winning goal! Thirty-three years later, that entire Summit Series team was inducted into the Canadian Sports Hall of Fame.

N is for a New York Yankee,
    who pitched his way to fame.
No hits, no runs, no errors—
    a World Series perfect game.

Pitching a perfect game—allowing not a single runner to reach base for an entire game—is one of the rarest feats in baseball. In fact, it has happened only once per every 11,000 or so big league games, which makes it all the more amazing that someone accomplished it during the pressure of the World Series. On October 8, 1956, New York Yankees righthander Don Larsen did it against the Brooklyn Dodgers. It was baseball's first perfect game in 34 years! Remarkably, Larsen lost more games than he won in his big league career.

N is also for Nolan Ryan's no-hitters. One of the fastest pitchers ever to set foot on a mound (his fastball was recorded at more than 100 mph), Ryan played for four teams in his remarkable 27-year major league career. Along the way, he set two records that may never be broken—5,714 strikeouts and an incredible seven no-hitters. He pitched his seventh and final no-hit game on May 1, 1991, when he was 44 years old!

N n

O is for the great Jesse Owens,
an Olympian who raised the bar.
All he needed was an opportunity,
and he became a global star.

Oo

The 1936 Summer Olympics were controversial because they were held in Berlin, Germany, where Nazi leader Adolph Hitler promoted a belief that all races were inferior to the German people. It would later require millions of soldiers to defeat him in his bid for world domination. But in those Olympic Games, one man proved the absurdity of Hitler's racist notions—Jesse Owens, the grandson of a slave.

Owens had already amazed American observers by establishing three world records and tying another in just 45 minutes during a college meet in 1935. But this time, he dazzled the world. First, he won a gold medal in the 100-meter dash... then in the long jump... then in the 200 meters... and finally in the 4x100-meter relay. It was a performance so remarkable and so symbolic that it was still celebrated 40 years later, when President Gerald Ford presented Owens with the Medal of Freedom, the highest honor given to a United States civilian.

The 85th match-up between storied college football rivals Stanford and California, on November 20, 1982, was an all-time classic. Stanford appeared to have won the game 20-19 after kicking a field goal with just four seconds left. But it wasn't over yet. California's Kevin Moen received the following kickoff and lateraled the ball to Richard Rodgers, who tossed it to Dwight Garner, who pitched it back to Rodgers, who lateraled it to Mariet Ford, who threw it blindly over his shoulder and back into the hands of Moen. By now, thinking the game was over, the Stanford band had marched onto the field. But Moen kept running—all the way to the end zone, where he barreled into a trombone player. When the touchdown was finally signaled, Cal radio announcer Joe Starkey put it best, calling it "the most amazing, sensational, heart-rending, exciting, thrilling finish in the history of college football!" As for that trombone player, his crumpled instrument is now on display at the College Football Hall of Fame.

P p

Four seconds left, five laterals,
and band members in the way.
P is for a classic ending
known simply as The Play.

Doug Flutie stood just under 5-foot-10, several inches shorter than most big-time quarterbacks, so people always thought he was too small to be a star. Boy did he prove them wrong! As a college quarterback, he won the Heisman Trophy as the nation's top player. He played in three different professional leagues, including the Canadian Football League, where he was named Most Outstanding Player a record six times. But his most memorable moment occurred on the day after Thanksgiving in 1984.

In a nationally televised game, Flutie's Boston College team trailed the University of Miami 45-41. With just six seconds remaining, Boston College was still 48 yards from the goal line. On the game's final play, Flutie scrambled away from the defense and lofted a perfect "Hail Mary" pass all the way downfield and right into the arms of receiver Gerard Phelan for a game-winning touchdown. The throw became so famous that the town of Natick, Massachusetts (Flutie's hometown) named a street in the quarterback's honor. They call it Flutie Pass.

Q
q

Q is for a Quarterback—
a little guy, Doug Flutie,
whose game-winning Hail Mary pass
was such a thing of beauty.

R is a Racehorse named Big Red,
a stallion of great renown,
who left the others far behind
and earned the Triple Crown.

Secretariat, a chestnut-colored horse known as Big Red, won 16 races in his 16-month career. In 1972, he won seven out of nine races and became the first two-year-old to be voted Horse of the Year. But he saved his most incredible performances for 1973, when he became the first horse in a quarter-century to win the three prestigious races that comprise horse racing's Triple Crown.

Jockey Ron Turcotte led Secretariat to victories in the first two jewels of the Crown, the Kentucky Derby and the Preakness Stakes. But it was the third race, the Belmont Stakes, that made Secretariat a legend. He won by an amazing 31 lengths (nearly 280 feet!), completing the $1\frac{1}{2}$-mile distance in a record time of 2 minutes, 24 seconds. It takes a lot of heart to compete at such a high level, and when Secretariat died in 1989, doctors discovered that this was literally true. His heart was almost twice the average size!

In 1968, 18-year-old swimmer Mark Spitz brashly predicted he would win six gold medals in the Summer Olympics. He didn't come close, taking home only two golds as part of American relay teams. But four years later, at the Summer Games in Munich, West Germany, Spitz exceeded even his own expectations. He won four individual events and was part of three winning relay teams—seven golds in all!

Spitz's total had been unsurpassed by any other athlete in a single Olympiad... until another swimming sensation came along. Michael Phelps (who won six golds and two bronze medals at the 2004 Olympics) was just about perfect at the 2008 Summer Games in Beijing, China. The 23-year-old American went home with eight gold medals, winning three team relays and five individual events (including the 100-meter butterfly, which he won by only $\frac{1}{100}$th of a second!) Along the way, Phelps set seven world records and an Olympic record. His 14 career gold medals are the most by any Olympian, and he may not be through yet! He plans to compete in the 2012 Summer Games.

S s

S is for two sensational Swimmers,
who surpassed one and all.
Seven gold medals! And then one more!
What a Summer Olympic haul!

T t

Nadia Comaneci was a tiny gymnast,
but she could really soar.
T? That stands for Ten,
the first-ever perfect score.

Nadia Comaneci began taking gymnastics lessons in her home country of Romania when she was six years old in 1968. By age 14, she was ready to dominate on the world's greatest athletic stage. At the 1976 Summer Olympics in Montreal, Canada, Comaneci performed such a flawless routine on the uneven bars that the judges gave her a score of 10.0. It was the first time in Olympic history that a perfect score had been awarded. In fact, the scoreboards were not even designed to display such a high score. Instead, they simply showed a 1.00! Over the next few days, she would receive six additional perfect scores, earning three gold medals and becoming the youngest Olympic all-around champion ever.

One person who was inspired by Nadia Comaneci was American gymnast Mary Lou Retton. At the 1984 Summer Olympics in Los Angeles, Retton scored perfect scores in her final two events (floor exercise and vault) to win the all-around title by just 0.05 points!

U is the ultimate Underdog.
Jason is his name.
He just wanted one chance to play,
then starred in a basketball game!

As manager of the Greece Athena High School basketball team in Greece, New York, Jason McElwain's job was to help run drills and hand out water bottles. While he may have dreamed about being a hoop superstar, it was unlikely. Jason was born with autism, a developmental disorder that affects his social skills. But in the last game of Greece Athena's 2006 regular season, the team's coach, Jim Johnson, decided to give the 17-year-old senior a parting gift. With only a few minutes left, he sent Jason into the game.

Jason missed his first two shots. Then he sank a long one... and another... and another. The crowd began to go wild. In all, he made seven baskets, including six three-pointers, scoring an amazing 20 points! When the buzzer sounded, the crowd stormed the court, and his teammates lifted Jason onto their shoulders. "I ended my career on the right note," Jason told a reporter after the game. "I was really hotter than a pistol!"

U u

March Madness brought pure joy
to a coach called Jimmy **V**
when a most unlikely college team
earned a stunning victory.

The finals of the 1983 NCAA men's basketball tournament appeared to be a mismatch. The University of Houston Cougars, nicknamed Phi Slamma Jamma, had won 25 games in a row and featured two future Hall of Famers, Hakeem Olajuwon and Clyde Drexler. Their opponent, the North Carolina State Wolfpack, had lost ten games that season. No team had ever won a national championship after losing that many times.

But to the surprise of everybody, the game was tied in the final seconds, and the Wolfpack had the ball. As the clock ticked down, Dereck Whittenburg heaved a desperate shot from 35 feet away. Could it be? No. Airball! Perhaps this wouldn't be one of the greatest upsets in college basketball history. But wait! The ball landed right in the hands of Whittenburg's teammate, Lorenzo Charles, who gently stuffed it through the hoop with one second remaining! While the fans stormed the court, Wolfpack coach Jim Valvano ran frantically through the crowds, searching for a player to hug.

W is for Wilma Rudolph,
who ran wondrously in Rome.
Where there's a will, there's a way.
She brought three gold medals home.

The odds were stacked against Wilma Rudolph. She was born into poverty in rural Tennessee, along with 21 brothers and sisters. She contracted several diseases as a child, including scarlet fever and polio, which left her nearly unable to use her left leg for several years. On top of it all, she grew up at a time when many women, especially African-American women, struggled to find opportunities and acceptance in sports. What were the chances that she would become a world famous Olympic sprinter?

But Rudolph was determined. Baseball pioneer Jackie Robinson told her, "Don't let anything, or anybody, keep you from running." So Rudolph became a track star in high school, in college, and finally in the Olympics. At the 1960 Summer Games in Rome, Italy, she won two individual events and was part of one victorious relay team, making her the first American woman to win three track and field gold medals. She was, said her former coach Nell Jackson, "beauty in motion."

W
W

At the Summer X Games,
the tension was extra-thick,
as halfpipe legend Tony Hawk
performed the ultimate skateboard trick.

When Tony Hawk was nine years old, his brother gave him a blue fiberglass banana board, his first true skateboard. By the time he was 14, Hawk was a professional skateboarder who would go on to be the best in the world, winning 73 pro contests. Known for inventing many moves on the halfpipe (tricks with names like backside varial and ollie-to-indy and lipslide revert), he always dreamed of landing one move in particular—the 900.

During the "Best Trick" competition at the 1999 X Games, Hawk tried over and over to complete the move, which requires a remarkable $2\frac{1}{2}$ rotations before landing on the halfpipe. He tried ten times and failed ten times, although twice he landed on his board only to have it slide out from under him. But on the eleventh attempt... success! The first ever 900! Tony decided to stop competing after that event. "What else is there?" he said. "The 900 was my goal."

Y is for the Yellow jersey
worn by a superman named Lance,
who overcame grave illness
to win the Tour de France.

American road racing cyclist Lance Armstrong had been hoping to perform well in the 1996 Tour de France, a grueling multi-stage road race that is one of the world's most difficult competitions. But he had to drop out early in the race after becoming ill. A few months later, he discovered he had cancer, and the disease had already spread to his lungs and brain. Armstrong underwent brain surgery and extensive chemotherapy, hoping he would survive the ordeal. But he didn't simply survive; he thrived!

Remarkably, Armstrong returned to participate in the 1999 Tour de France. Even more amazing, he won it, receiving the yellow jersey that goes to the winner. He went on to win the event seven times in a row, a new record! After his seventh victory in 2005, he retired from racing (for awhile at least). However, he is still making news with his crusade against cancer. His "Livestrong" bracelets have raised more than $60 million to battle the disease.

Y
y

Z On college basketball's biggest stage,
is the clock ticking down to Zero.
A full-court pass, a catch, a shot.
Swish! We have ourselves a hero.

The 1991 NCAA men's basketball tournament game between the Duke Blue Devils and the Kentucky Wildcats matched two of the sport's most successful programs. The winner would move on to the Final Four, and both teams wanted it badly. The game went into overtime, and the lead changed hands several times. With 14 seconds left, Duke took a 102-101 lead. But with 2.2 seconds left Kentucky went ahead 103-102. Duke called a time out and set up one final, improbable play.

Duke's Christian Laettner, who had already been virtually flawless, connecting on all nine of his shot attempts and all ten of his free throws, stood not far from the free throw line. From the baseline nearly 80 feet away, his teammate Grant Hill threw an overhand pass right into Laettner's hands. Laettner turned, dribbled once, jumped and released a 17-foot shot, just before the buzzer sounded. Swish! Victory! It was a fitting end to what Duke point guard Bobby Hurley called "the best game I've ever been a part of."

Z z

A Timeline of Amazing Moments

1926 — Gertude Ederle swims English Channel

1936 — Jesse Owens wins four gold medals

1946 — Jackie Robinson plays first professional game

1954 — Roger Bannister runs first four-minute mile

1956 — Don Larsen pitches World Series perfect game

1960 — Wilma Rudolph runs to three gold medals

1968 — Bob Beamon's record-setting long jump

1969 — the Amazin' Mets win World Series

1972 — Mark Spitz swims to seven gold medals

1972 — Franco Harris makes Immaculate Reception

1973 — Secretariat wins horse racing's Triple Crown

1973 — Billie Jean King wins the Battle of the Sexes

1976 — David Pearson wins the Duel at Daytona

1976 — Nadia Comaneci records a perfect 10

1980 — the Miracle on Ice

1982 — Cal pulls off "The Play" against Stanford

1983 — North Carolina State stuns the basketball world

1984 — Mary Lou Retton wins gymnastics gold medal

1984 — Doug Flutie's Hail Mary pass

1986 — Jack Nicklaus wins his final Masters

1988 — Kirk Gibson's World Series home run

1991 — Nolan Ryan pitches seventh no-hitter

1991 — Christian Laettner's buzzer-beating shot

1997 — Tiger Woods wins his first Masters

1998 — Michael Jordan's title-winning jump shot

1999 — Lance Armstrong wins his first Tour de France

1999 — Brandi Chastain's kick wins World Cup

1999 — Tony Hawk performs a 900

2006 — Jason McElwain's 20-point basketball game

2008 — Michael Phelps wins eight Olympic medals